Diver's pearls

Welcome! Come and learn some pearls of wisdom about cursive handwriting, and Australia's cultural heritage.

My background

Name: ______________________

School: ______________________

Date of birth: ______________________

Place of birth: ______________________

Hobbies: ______________________

Interests: ______________________

____

____

In this space, paste a picture of something that is of cultural or historical significance to your family. It could be a letter, family heirloom or a treasured memento of your family's history.

Revision

Printing letters and numerals

Practise the lower-case letters.

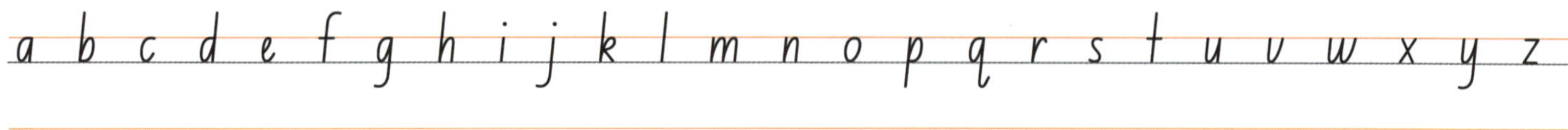

Write the capital letters.

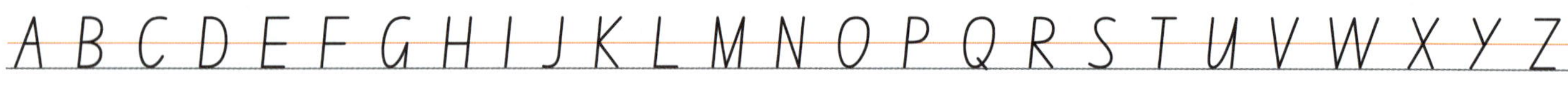

Practise these numerals.

Diver's pearls

When the letter u follows q, the two letters join like this: qu.

The cursive alphabet

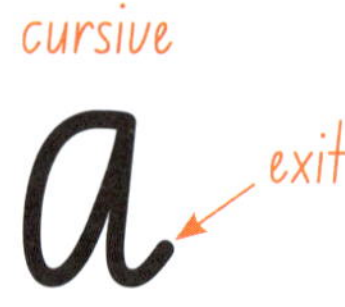

Write the cursive alphabet.

abcdefghijklmnopqurstuvwxyz

abcdefghijklmnopqurstuvwxyz

Cursive letter size and direction

Sort the cursive alphabet letters into these categories according to their size. Write each letter once only.

Head and body letters (6 letters)

Body letters (14 letters)

Body and tail letters (5 letters)

Head, body and tail letter (1 letter)

Write these words in the correct column.

mother even screamed swimming games rain

Words with body letters only	Words with head and body letters	Words with body and tail letters

Write the cursive letters that are formed in a **clockwise direction.** Clockwise letters follow the clockwise movement shown in the pattern.

hm

Now write the cursive letters that are formed in an **anti-clockwise direction**. Anti-clockwise letters follow the anti-clockwise movement shown in the pattern.

yu

These letters flow in both directions.

g s y

These are straight-line letters.

i t l x z

Diagonal joins

in eu

Practise these diagonal joins.

ur an in es er am tu us ip en ey ar

ix ti he te cu mi at ly hi ee ke me ay nu

Australia culture discrimination happened Chinese

Diver's pearls

Diagonal joins are the most common joins in cursive handwriting.

Now practise these sentences with diagonal joins.

During the gold rush years, many Chinese gold-seekers came to Australia by ship. When they arrived, they lived and worked together, partly due to discrimination. Today, the influence these people had on culture and foods is part of our heritage.

OXFORD UNIVERSITY PRESS

Diagonal joins to ascenders

Retrace a little on the way down.

Copy these letters with extended exits.

t e a i u l c k   t e a i u l c k

Now use the sweeping movement to write diagonal joins to ascenders.

th et al it ul el ub ut at cl ch lt nk

the they together Australia ship teams

tent generally healthy population nationality immigrate

Diver's pearls

The crossbar on t needs to be level with the top of body letters.

Practise these diagonal joins to ascenders.

Some Chinese people who came to the mines started small businesses, grew fruit and vegetables in market gardens, and healed people with herbal medicines. These activities improved the health of miners.

Diagonal joins: fluency patterns

Trace the incense smoke, then try the letter patterns. While completing the letter patterns, try to keep the movements parallel. When you have finished, check your slope consistency by extending the incense sticks down to the pattern.

Shoulder letters and drop-in joins

slide left

Extend exit, lift, and drop in shoulder letter.

Diver's pearls

Shoulder letters all start by sliding left along the top line. When following a diagonal join, the shoulder letter is dropped into place.

Copy the shoulder letters.

a c d g q a c d g q a c d g q a c d g q a c d g q a c d g q

Write these drop-in joins. The dot shows you when to lift the pencil.

na ma ic ud aq ug id eg ec nd iq da ig ed uc ag

Practise these drop-in joins.

incense light hanging lasted fantastic aroma

selected opaque candles started handy

suddenly daylight wondering mystical shadows

For the word below, draw a dot above each of the drop-in joins.

misunderstanding

Practise writing the word, using two colours. Change colours each time you come to a drop-in join.

Drop-in joins

Touch the diagonal exit here.

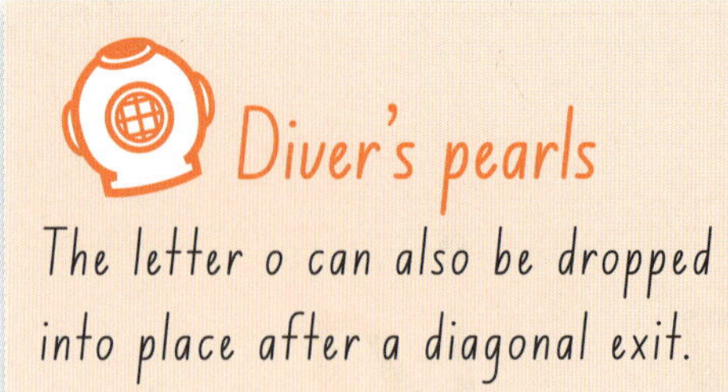

Copy the text to practise drop-in joins to anti-clockwise letters.

In Vietnamese Buddhist temples you may be lucky enough to see

the large incense coils hanging from the ceilings. Visitors are

invited to purchase a coil and write on the red tag, which

then hangs with the coil. The coils are so large they are

said to burn for up to a month.

Finish the coil patterns.

Horizontal joins

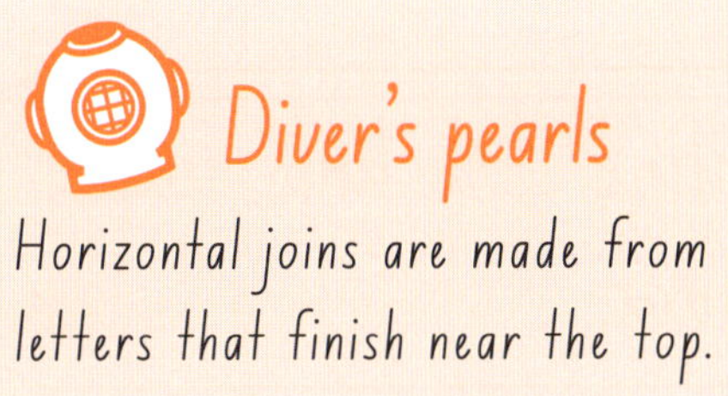

Horizontal joins are made from letters that finish near the top.

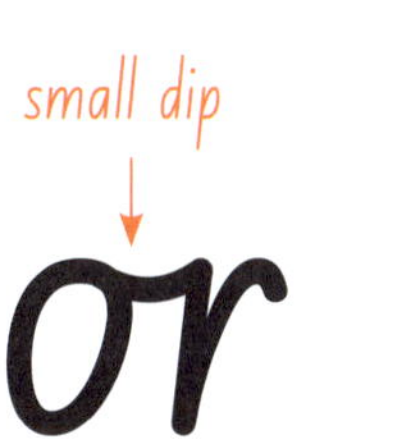

o r v w   o r v w   o r v w   o r v w   o r v w   o r v w   o r v w

Practise these horizontal joins.

or vs wi ru ou vi ow ox om op ru rm

ri oi on ov wn wr rr og wd ot wt

burning fragrance now meditation ground down hope

tranquil old harmony warmth ownership smoke

Top finishers to e

Do you remember that top finishers dip further to join to e? Practise these.

slightly bigger dip

oe

oe we ve re   oe we ve re   oe we ve re   oe we ve re

went received reward discover clever westerly five beware

lower fire arrive does lived forever more weekend

Assessment: joins

Write these sentences in cursive.

Foundation handwriting is a quick, legible style of writing. Join lines need to be as straight as possible to keep your handwriting neat.

Write the diagonal join pairs from the text above.

un at

Write the drop-in join pairs from the text above.

nd io

Write the pairs that have a horizontal join.

ou on

Circle the diagonal joins and underline the drop-in joins.

ug ne ac ie nd le ag aq mi uk th cc un ec em

Self-assessment

Assess your joins.

☐ Lack-lustre performance ☐ Good display ☐ It's a pearler!

Teacher

Fluency Joins

Fluency joins from b, p and s

Retrace the bottom of the letter.

Diver's pearls

For fluency joins from b, p and s, retrace the bottom of the letter before exiting from the baseline to make a join.

Practise these fluency joins using b, p and s.

be bu bi bl br ba bb pe pu pr pl pi

pa pp se si sc sr st sl su sa ss

pearling industry fishing Japanese boats

bags apparatus vessels bends sharks shells

snorkel oysters buttons boats brave paid suits

Make your own words using fluency joins.

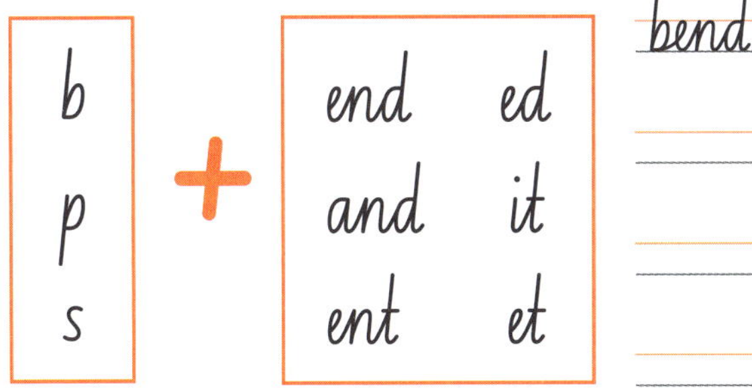

bend

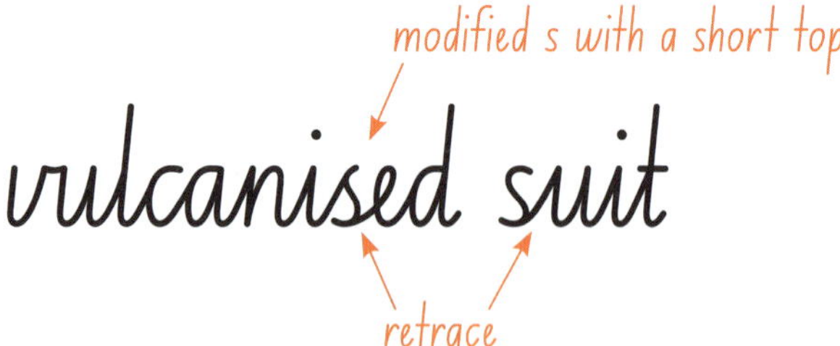

Fluency joins help us to write faster. Using a modified s after a diagonal join also helps to speed up our writing.

Practise the modified s after a diagonal join.

as es is us ls ms ns bs ps ts

Practise these fluency joins.

Pearling commenced in Broome, Western Australia, in the 1850s.

The divers were mostly Japanese. The diving suits worn were

vulcanised canvas with massive bronze helmets. Divers also wore

lead-weighted boots. They spent hours

looking through thick faceplates and

scooping up oysters. Divers were paid

by the number of shells they collected.

Fluency joins from capital letters

Joining from some capital letters can be used to increase speed and fluency. Try these joins.

Au Mi Co Fi Ro Ha Ke Qu Us

Australian Mr Mikimoto Company First Rough

Harbour Keshi pearls Quickly Usually

Who was Mr Mikimoto?

Try these fluency join patterns. Remember to keep the downstrokes parallel.

Au

Ke

Consolidation of fluency joins

Copy these sentences.

A glossary is an alphabetical collection or list of specialist terms and their meanings. The glossary below relates to the history of the pearling industry.

The meanings of the words in the box are listed below and on the next page.

- Write the words in the box beside their meanings.
- Copy the words and the meanings.

tender, oyster, cyclone, Mr Mikimoto, lugger, the bends, vulcanised

______________________ : painful condition experienced often by divers; caused by too much nitrogen in the blood. This condition sometimes results in the death of the diver.

______________________ : large boat used for pearling. It has two masts and two sails.

_______________: violent wind and rain storm.

_______________: the person who helps and looks after the diver while they are under water.

_______________: considered the father of the cultured pearl industry.

_______________: strengthened material such as canvas.

_______________: irregular, rough shellfish with two parts. It is where a pearl is formed.

Copy these words to practise fluency joins. See if you can increase your speed and fluency on the second and third copy lines.

population descendants British respected between past

Copy these sentences.

Australia is a multicultural nation. First Nations peoples have hundreds of cultural groups, and have been here for thousands of years. More recently, colonisation and immigration have both changed Australia's population. Australia's population is made up of individuals from over 200 countries, making us one of the world's most culturally diverse nations. Nearly one in four people living in Australia was born overseas.

Copy these sentences to continue practising fluency joins.

Australian Indigenous art has existed for over 30 000 years. Rock carvings and body painting have evolved into many different art forms, which differ between cultures and regions. Today, Indigenous art is created on mediums such as paper, canvas, glass, wood, ceramics and fabrics. For Indigenous Australians, art is an important way of connecting with their history, ancestors and the land. Australian Indigenous art is admired and respected all around the world.

Writing with speed

Work with a partner to time your writing.

Diver's pearls

Even when writing quickly, it is important to maintain legibility so that others can read your writing.

Write the word 'pearling' in cursive with fluency joins.
How many times can you write the word in one minute?

☐ Prediction ☐ Actual number

pearling

If you printed, do you think the number would increase or decrease?
Print the word 'pearling' as many times as you can in one minute.

☐ Prediction ☐ Actual number

pearling

When writing in capitals, do you think you write faster or slower?
Write 'pearling' in capital letters to find out.

☐ Prediction ☐ Actual number

PEARLING

Assessment: fluency joins

Rewrite these words, adding the fluency joins where necessary.

sisters robbers slept scooped both space

Rewrite these words, adding the fluency joins from capital letters where possible.

Australian Brazilian Chinese Dutch English French German

Hungarian Indian Japanese Kenyan Lebanese Maltese

Rewrite these words, adding all possible joins.

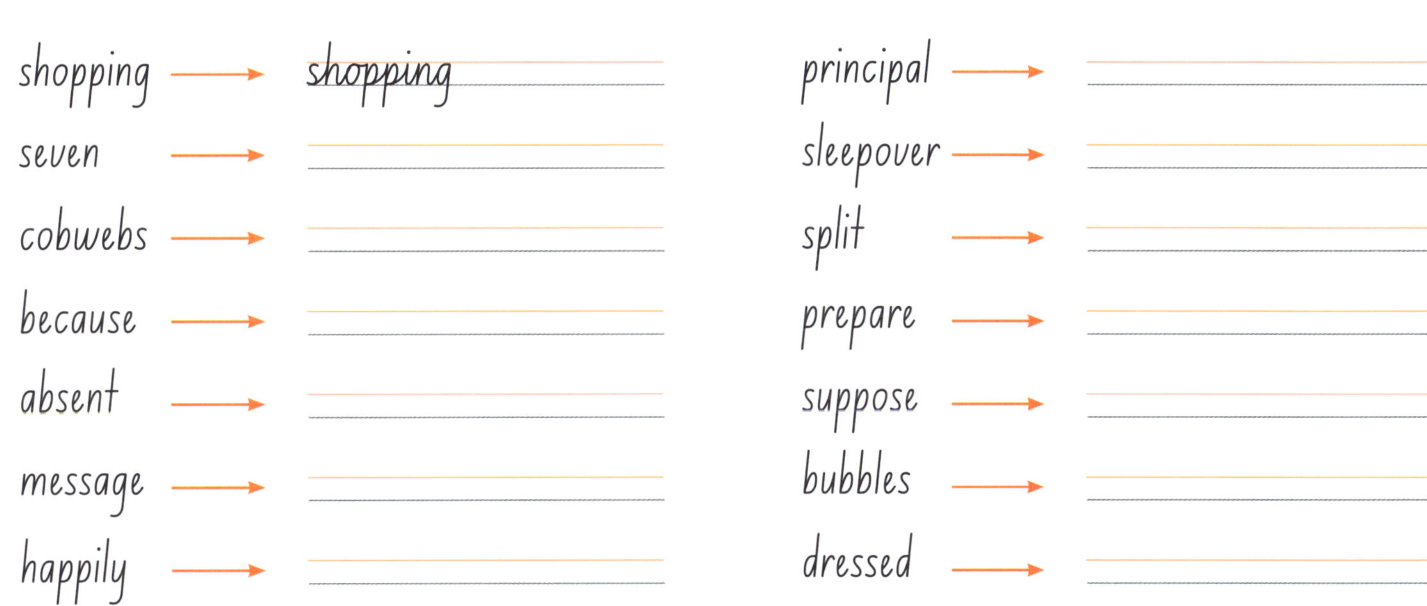

Self-assessment

Assess your fluency joins.

☐ Lack-lustre performance

☐ Good display

☐ It's a pearler!

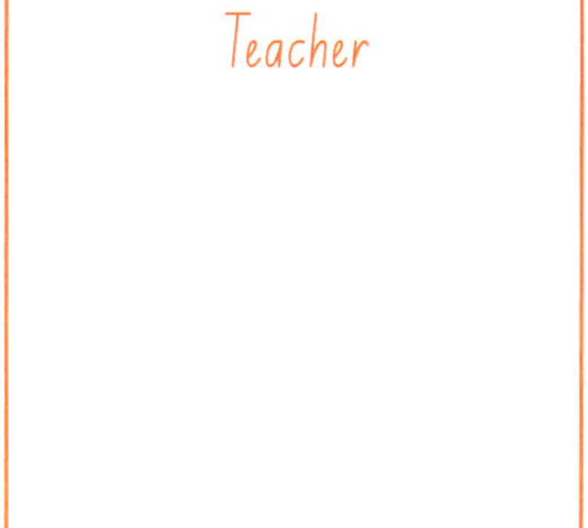

Slope consistency

Copy this text.

To keep your handwriting legible, your slope should be consistent. Right-handed writers usually slope their writing to the right. Left-handers may prefer to slope their writing to the left.

Write these words, then add in the slope lines. Are they parallel?

handwriting usually legible consistent slope
hands keep writers left should their the

Copy the first row five times, increasing the speed of your writing each time. Then check your slope by ruling lines along the downstrokes.

slope slope slope slope slope

Diver's pearls

Locate the slope card in the back of this book. Place it under this page and use it as a guide to help keep the slope of your writing consistent.

Write this word, using the slope lines as a guide.

immigration

Write the word and then add in the slope lines.

immigration

Circle the words with an inconsistent slope. Then, write all of the words using a consistent slope.

society enrich diverse cultures food family

music history education nation modern skills

Diver's pearls

Remember to use the slope card in the back of this book to check your slope consistency. Place the slope card under your writing as a guide.

Copy this text. Maintain a consistent slope.

Eddie Koiki Mabo was a Torres Strait Islander who campaigned for Indigenous land rights. On 3 June 1992, five months after Eddie Mabo had passed away, it was ruled that Australia was not 'terra nullius' (no man's land) in 1788 when Europeans began colonising the land. The decision, commonly called 'Mabo', recognised Aboriginal and Torres Strait Islanders' right to land that had since been occupied by European colonisers.

Diver's pearls

Keeping your spacing even between letters and words will make your writing more legible for your audience.

cultural contributions 

cultural contributions 

As you copy this text try to develop an even spacing between letters that feels comfortable for your writing hand.

During the 1920s and 1930s, many southern Europeans arrived

in Australia. Some worked as labourers in remote rural areas,

and helped to set up Australia's rural industries, roads and

railways. In capital cities, Italian stonemasons built public

buildings and residential homes. Across Australia, some Greek

immigrants opened cafes, giving other Australians a taste of modern

European food and culture.

Keep your spacing even as you copy these words.

Second World War Jewish refugees Latvia Ukraine Austria

Poland Slovakia Czech Republic Bulgaria Hungary Lithuania

Copy the sentences, taking special care with your spacing.

Thousands of Jewish people came to Australia because of the Second World War. They were refugees who had fled Nazi rule. After the war, about 170 000 Europeans who had lost their homes immigrated to Australia. They brought with them their education, skills and unique cultures. They helped to improve our society.

Speed Loops and Fluency

Speed loops from g, j and y

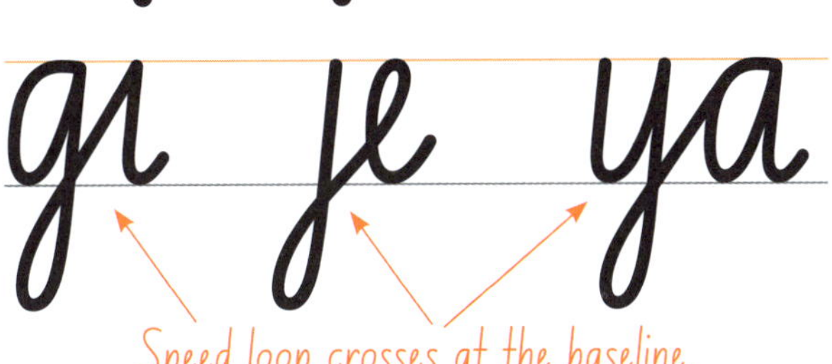

Diver's pearls

Speed loops can be used to increase the speed and fluency of your writing. Speed loops from g, j and y should cross at the baseline. If g, j or y are at the end of a word, they do not need a loop as they are not joining to another letter.

Practise these speed loops from g.

gi gi ge ge go go gr gr ga ga

girl great going good green grass gate games

Practise these speed loops from j.

ju ju ja ja je je jo jo ji ji

jump jam jar jig jet just jug injury jitters

Practise these speed loops from y.

ya ya yo yo yu yu yi yi ye ye

yesterday young yummy yard typing year yet

Speed loops to ascenders: b, h, k and l

Diver's pearls

Speed loops can also be added when joining to ascenders b, h, k and l. Speed loops to ascenders should cross at the top body line.

Speed loop crosses at the top body line.

lb th

Copy these speed loops to b.

ab yb ib kb eb ub ob rb ub wb lb

able nibble pebble gobble grub somebody gibberish

Copy these speed loops to h.

th ah gh eh sh ch ph oh wh

thick laugh shout church phone which

Copy these speed loops to k.

ck ok nk uk ek rk lk ok sk

snack pink week talk risk nickel pocket

Copy these speed loops to l.

al cl el dl gl il pl rl ol wl

always walk happily chocolate should replied

More about speed loops to ascenders

Copy these words with speed loops to ascenders.

clothes although pearl blast riddle glue

Copy this speed loop pattern.

lyy lyy

Diver's pearls

No loop is used if a word begins with b, h, k or l. Loops are only used when joining to these letters.

Copy these words. Remember not to use a loop for words beginning with b, h, k and l.

b biscuit → ib nibble

h house → sh shoulder

k kite → ck knock

l lamp → il bill

The letter f

Diver's pearls

The letter f changes depending on its position within a word. At the start of a word, f has a loop from its tail but no crossbar. In the middle of a word, there is a speed loop to the head of f and also from the tail of f. At the end of a word, f has a speed loop to its head and finishes with a crossbar.

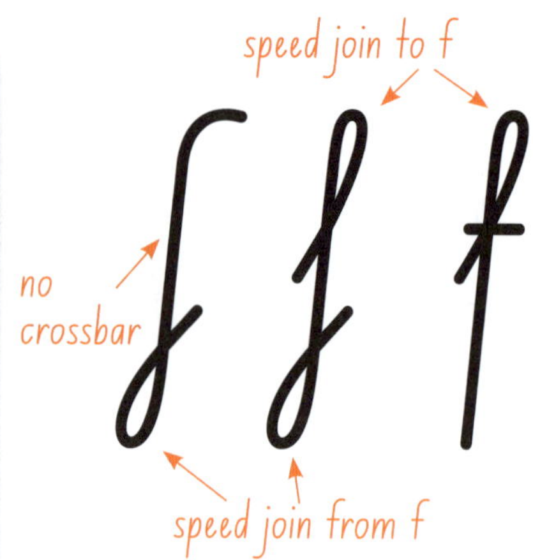

Practise writing the letter f at the beginning of a word.

fa fa fi fi fu fu fl fl fo fo

fantastic finally footy famous first

Practise writing these joins to f when f is in the middle of the word.

aft aft oft oft ufu ufu efi efi efo efo

after often life beautiful lofty before

Practise these joins to f when f is the last letter of a word.

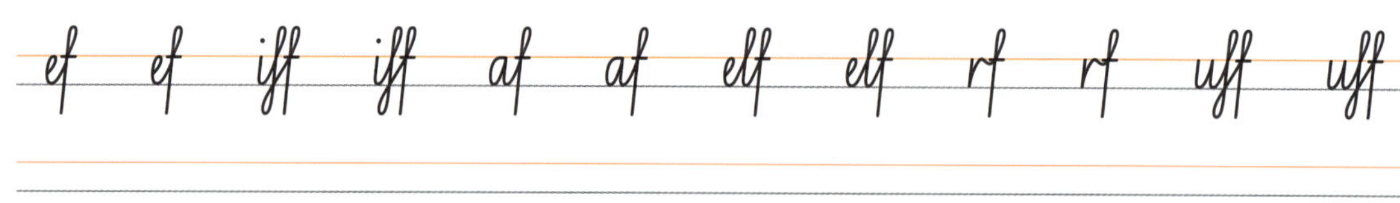

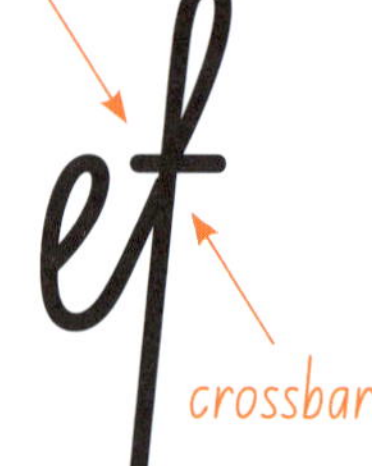

def diff loaf shelf surf sniff

Finish this pattern.

Speed loop fluency trials

How many times can you print the word below in one minute?

always

☐ Times

Now write the word in cursive, without using speed loops.

always

☐ Times

Write the word in cursive, using speed loops.

always

☐ Times

Compare your results. In which script were you able to write the word the most times?

Read this sentence and try to memorise it. Using cursive, write the sentence as many times as you can in one minute. At the end, count how many words you wrote.

Diving down deep into the sea was very dangerous for pearl divers.

First try: __________

Second try: __________

Building fluency using speed loops

How much do you know about Foundation Cursive script? Select the correct definition from the box and write it beside the matching term, using Foundation Cursive script with fluency joins and speed loops.

- the tall part of letters such as b, k, l, h
- the ability to produce handwriting that is clear and easy to read
- the tail of letters that extend below the baseline
- letters that flow in the opposite direction to the movement of hands on a clock
- the smooth, easy flow when forming letters in handwriting
- the loops formed to and from ascenders or descenders to enhance joining fluency
- letters that flow in the same direction as the movement of hands on a clock

anti-clockwise letters:

ascenders:

clockwise letters:

descenders

fluency:

legibility:

speed loops:

Speed loop fluency with high-frequency words

Check your speed loop fluency with these high-frequency words from the **Oxford Wordlist**.

years great everyone dragon suddenly

looking shopping bought walking everything

finally through sleep why happily well

playing dark where shark always beautiful

which night school really while when

think watched finished teacher help

Rewrite these high-frequency words with fluency joins and speed loops.

goal kick boys could anything whole looking

through walking always girls years beach

Assessment: speed loops

Copy these sentences with speed loops. Take care with all the speed loops.

The Aboriginal flag was designed by Harold Thomas. It was first flown on National Aborigines Day in Adelaide on 12 July 1971. The flag is divided horizontally into halves. The black represents the Aboriginal people. The red represents the red earth, red ochre and Aboriginal people's spiritual relationship to the land. The yellow represents the sun, which gives life and is a protector.

Assess the fluency and legibility of your speed loops.

☐ Lack-lustre performance

☐ Good display

☐ It's a pearler!

Choosing a Script to Match a Purpose

Which script?

Copy this text using speed loops and fluency joins.

Different scripts are used at different times. Choose your script to suit the purpose of your writing. Cursive is the most appropriate for everyday writing.

Capital letters and print script are used when labelling and filling in forms.

Complete the table using the appropriate script.

CAPITAL LETTERS: for labelling maps	Print: for labelling diagrams, maps and sub-headings	Cursive: for everyday handwriting
AUSTRALIA	Canberra	Australian
CHINA	Beijing	Chinese
VIETNAM	Hanoi	Vietnamese
JAPAN	Tokyo	Japanese
INDIA	New Delhi	Indian

Matching script and purpose

Diver's pearls

Practise your speed loops for handwriting fluency. Cursive script with speed loops is the most appropriate choice for everyday writing. Make sure you maintain good posture, especially when writing for long periods of time.

Copy these sentences. Remember to maintain good posture.

Have you got your posture under control? If your posture is balanced, writing is easier and legibility can be maintained for longer. Sometimes we write for short periods away from a table, but for prolonged periods, choose an appropriately sized desk and chair.

Print these labels on the correct line.

Desk height should be appropriate.

Sit well back in the chair.

Keep your feet flat.

Slant the paper.

Diver's pearls

Print script is best for labelling diagrams.

Labelling maps and diagrams

Colour the flags.

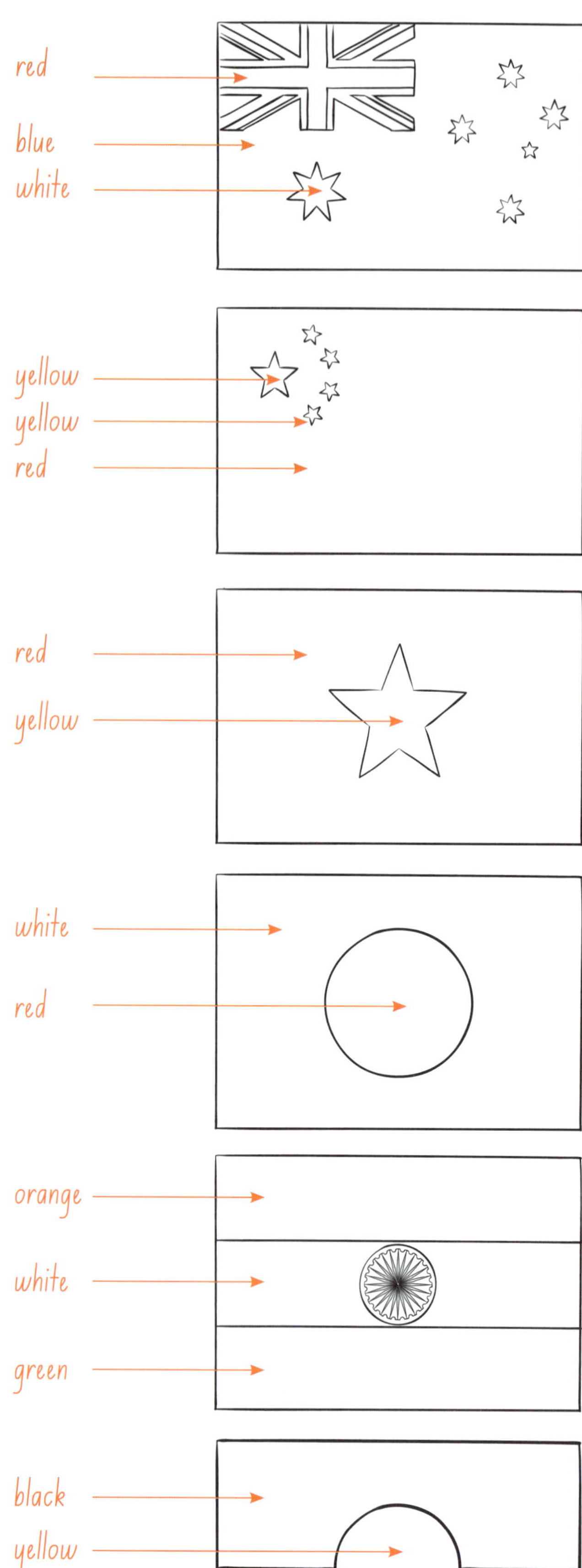

Print the labels.

AUSTRALIA

red blue white

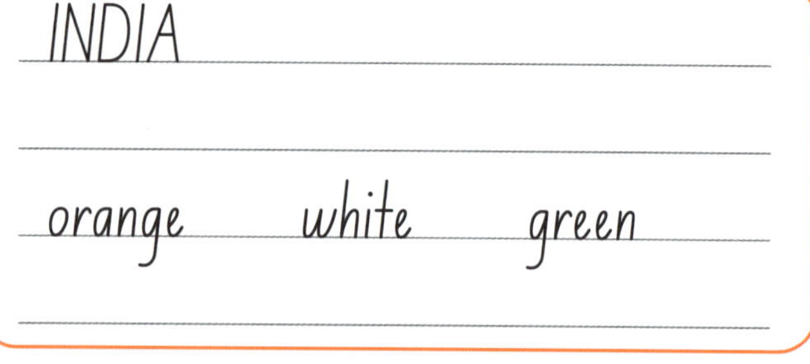

ABORIGINAL

black yellow red

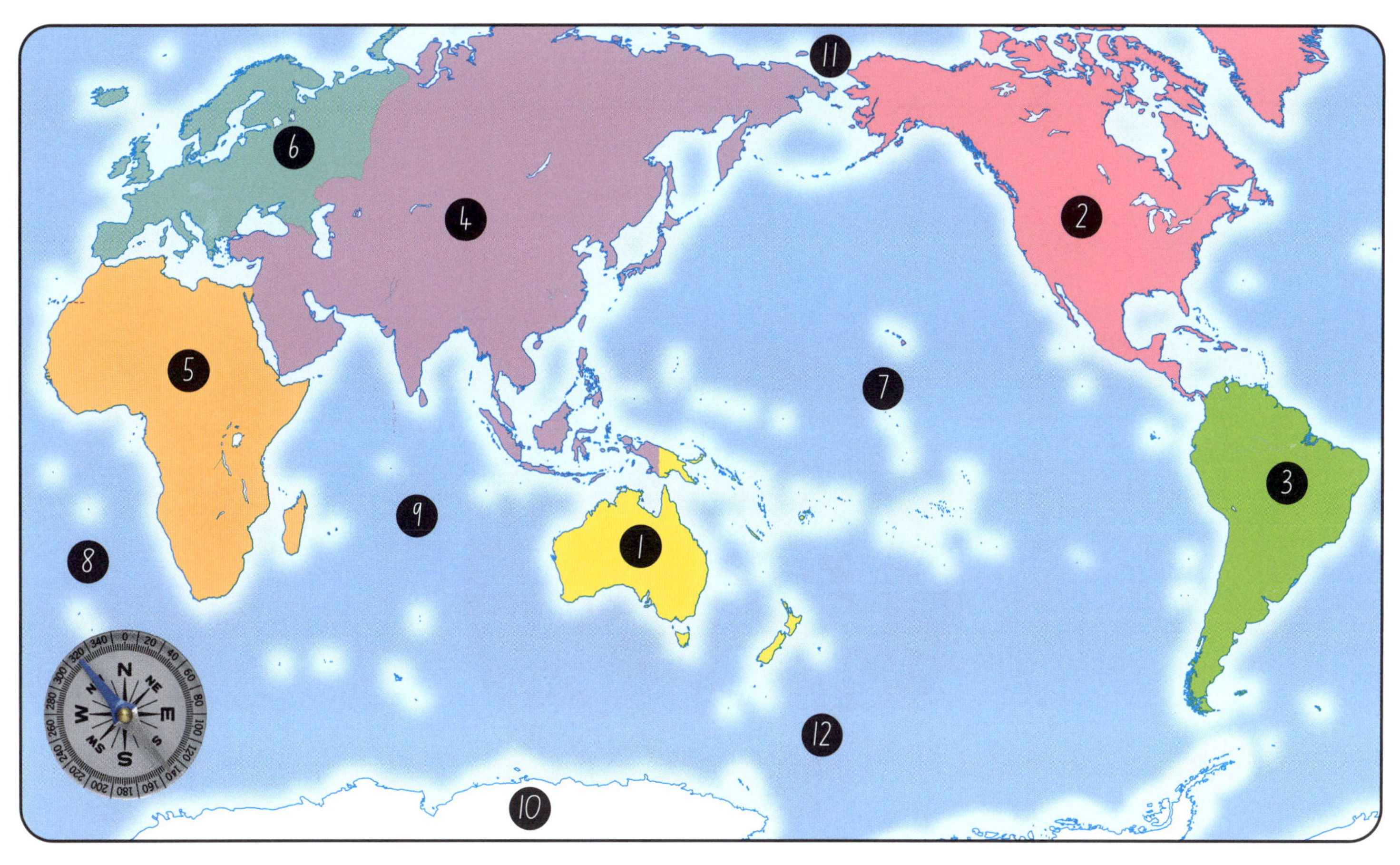

Practise your print script. Write the names of these continents and oceans beside their matching numbers. Use an atlas if you need help.

North America
South America
Europe
Africa

Asia
Australia
Antarctica
Indian Ocean

Pacific Ocean
Atlantic Ocean
Southern Ocean
Arctic Ocean

1 ________________
2 ________________
3 ________________
4 ________________
5 ________________
6 ________________

7 ________________
8 ________________
9 ________________
10 ________________
11 ________________
12 ________________

If you were travelling from Europe, in which direction would you travel to reach Australia?

____

Label the compass points using print script.

Now write the compass points in cursive.

Self-assessment

Assess your print accuracy.

☐ Lack-lustre performance

☐ Good display

☐ It's a pearler!

Teacher

The flourished alphabet

Diver's pearls

The flourished alphabet is great for presenting text in a decorative way. Use it to add a special touch to:

- project headings
- invitations
- birthday cards
- letters.

Just remember that it is not quick to write, so it is not ideal for everyday writing.

Eight letters change to form the flourished alphabet. Practise writing these.

slide left

b b b b b b b b b b b b b b b b b b b

slide left

h h h h h h h h h h h h h h h h h h h

slide left

k k k k k k k k k k k k k k k k k k k

slide left

l l l l l l l l l l l l l l l l l l l

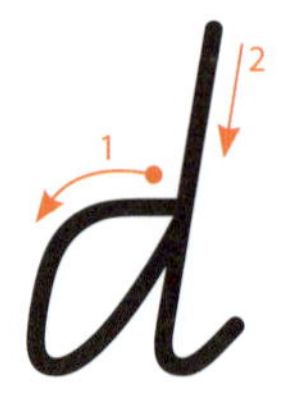

d d d d d d d d d d d d d d d d d d d

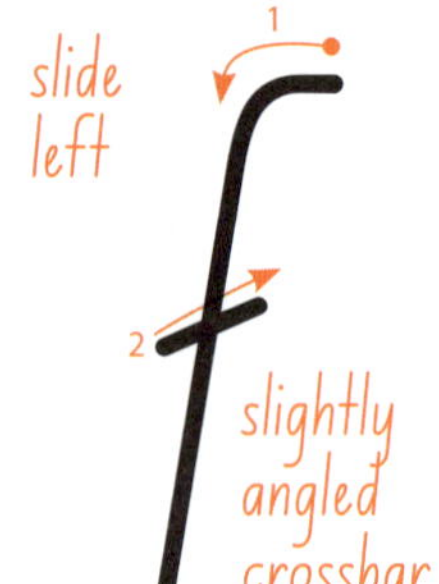

f f f f f f f f f f f f f f f f f f f

p p p p p p p p p p p p p p p p p p p

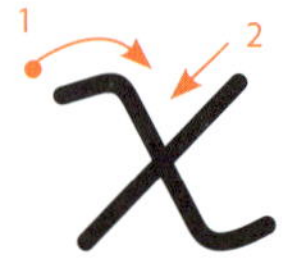

x x x x x x x x x x x x x x x x x x x

Copy these letters.

b d f h k l p x   b d f h k l p x

Write these words, using flourished handwriting.

boxing deal faith finished foxes health help

heal keep kettle knight leap laugh locked

made panda people pamper selfish teach x-ray

Flourished capitals

Write the flourished capitals.

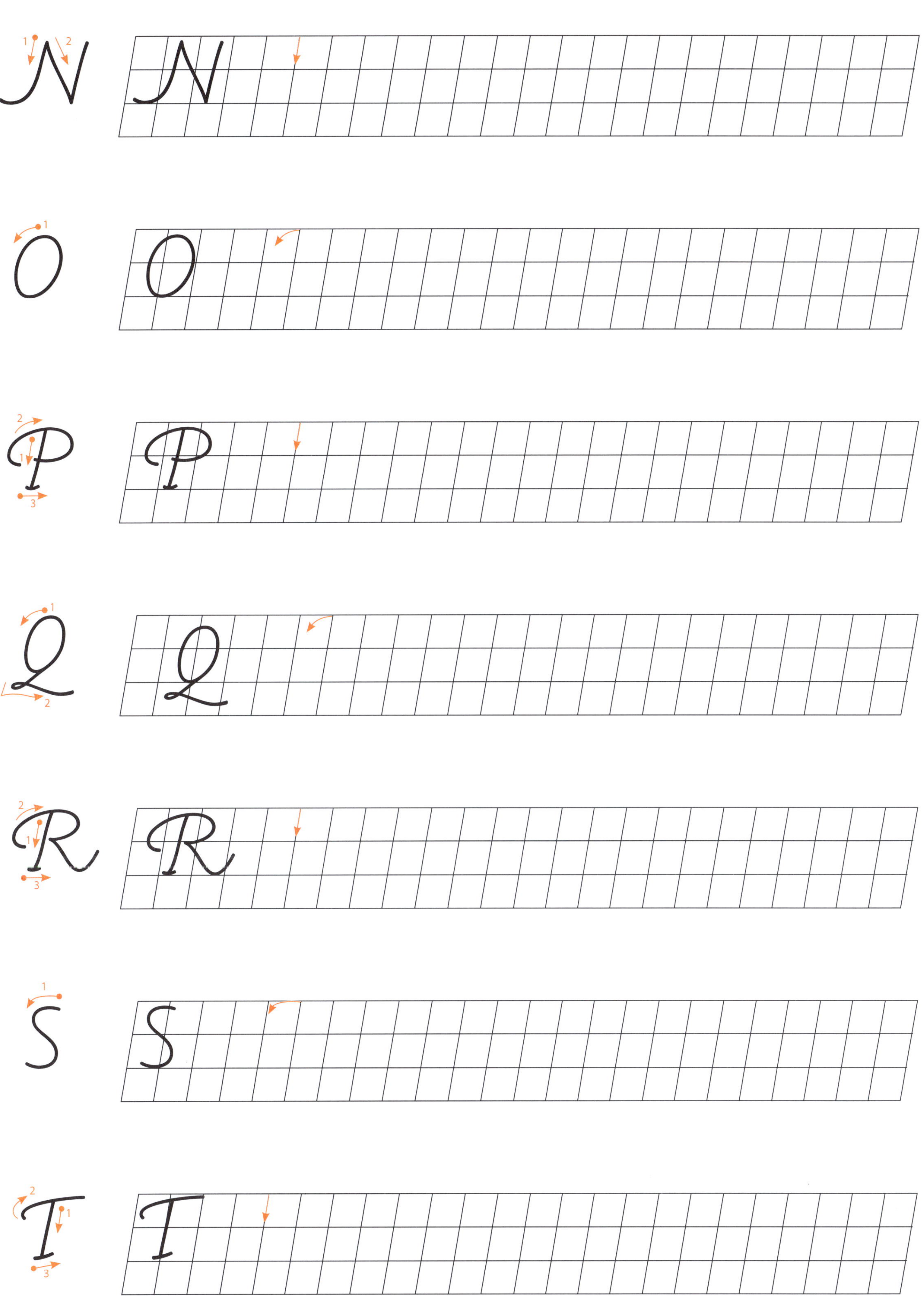
N
O
P
Q
R
S
T

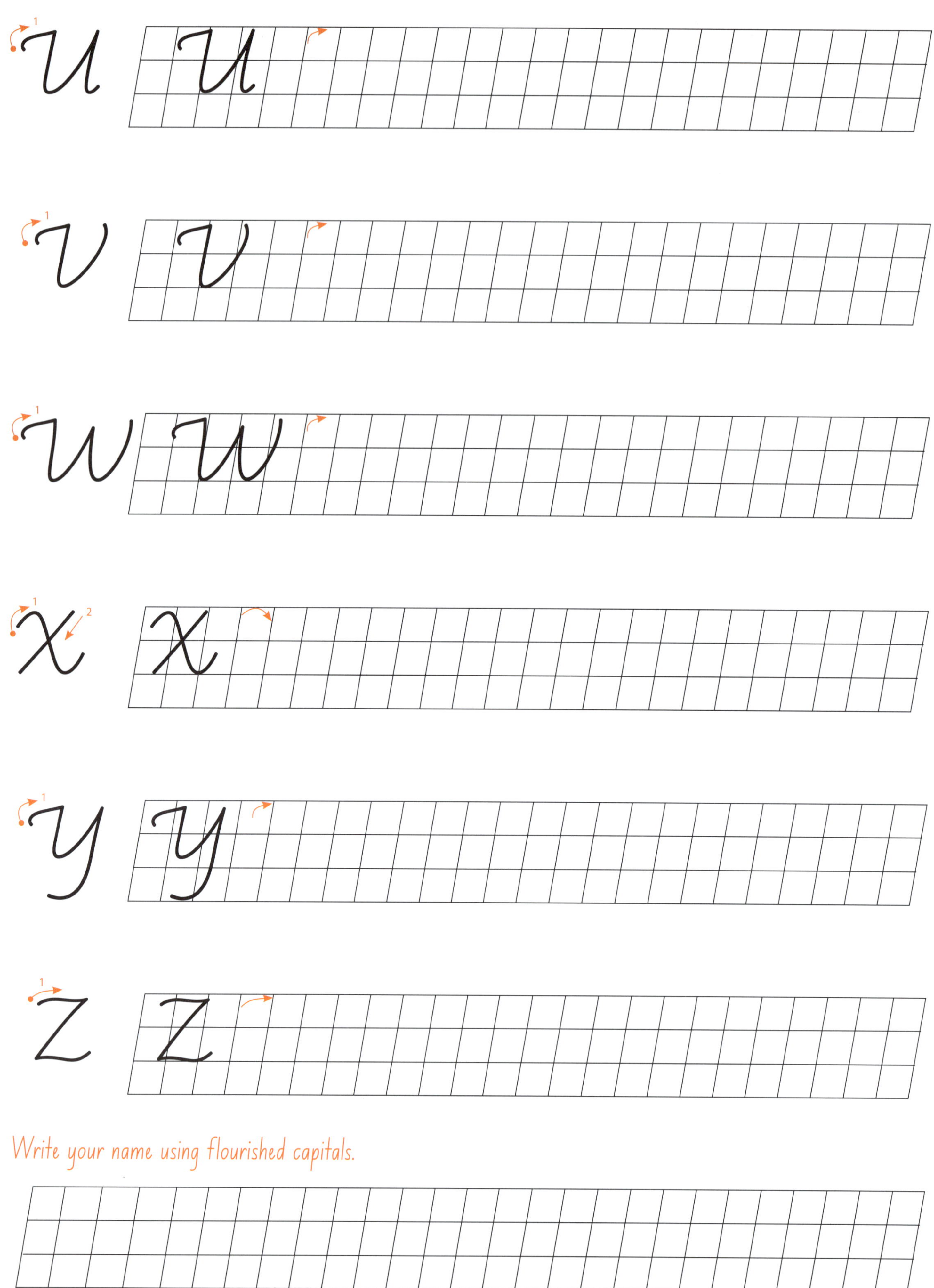

Write your name using flourished capitals.

Add flourished capitals to these travel book titles and authors' names. The number in brackets tells you how many flourished capitals are needed.

(4) travel the world by ali saad

(4) asian highlights by susan moon

(4) trips on a budget by sam rawson

(6) see the world on your own by harper dee

(6) ten top european destinations by lucy harris

(5) nile travel guide by alex mostafa

(6) chinese travel map by sue lee leung

(5) luxury travel in france by marie kilmore

Diver's pearls

The flourished alphabet is sometimes used as a decorative font on book covers.

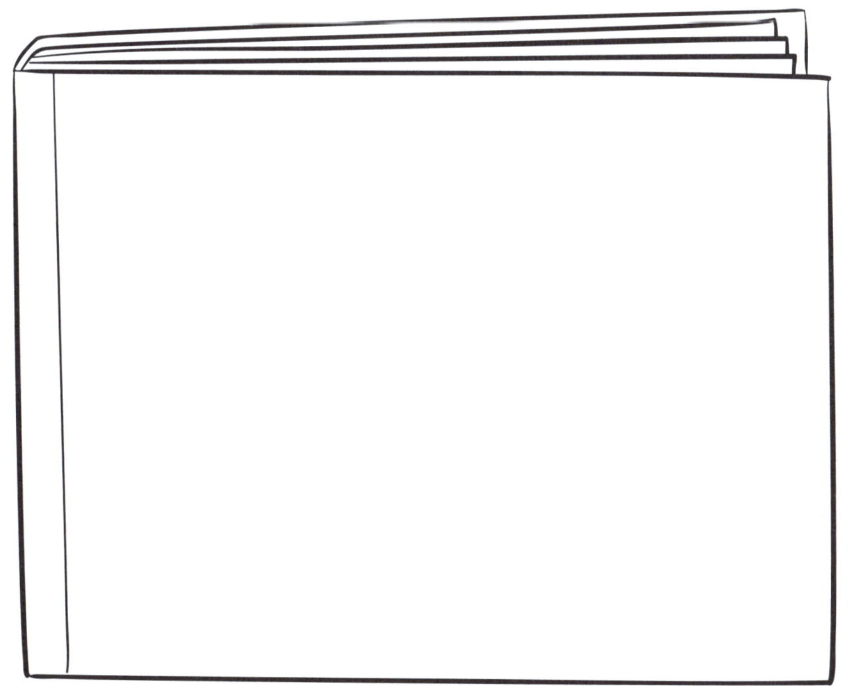

Use flourished writing to add your own book title and author name to this cover.

Practising flourished letters

Using the flourished alphabet, address this envelope to:

Julia Thomas
16 Martin Street
Ascot QLD 4007

Write this message to Julia, using flourished letters.

Having a great time visiting my nonna in Italy.
I am learning a lot about my culture. Today she is teaching me how to make pasta!
Love Emma

Imagine that you are a gold-digger working on the Australian goldfields during the 1850s. Using the flourished alphabet, write a letter to your family and tell them about your experiences on the goldfields.

Alphabet review

Copy models of each alphabet script in this book.

Print

a b c d e f g h i j k l m n o p q r s t u v w x y z

Cursive

abcdefghijklmnopqurstuvwxyz abcdefghijklmnopqurstuvwxyz

Cursive with fluency joins

abcdefghijklmnopqurstuvwxyz abcdefghijklmnopqurstuvwxyz

Cursive with fluency joins and speed loops

abcdefghijklmnopqurstuvwxyz abcdefghijklmnopqurstuvwxyz

Capital letters

A B C D E F G H I J K L M N O P Q R S T U V W X Y Z

Flourished capital letters

A B C D E F G H I J K L M

N O P Q R S T U V W X Y Z

Flourished lower-case letters

b d f h k l p x b d f h k l p x